BLUEGRASS UKULELE

ARRANGED BY FRED SOKOLOW

Contents

To access audio visit:
www.halleonard.com/mylibrary
Enter Code
1556-8556-0302-6932

The Recording
Ukulele, Mandolin, Guitar, and Vocals—Fred Sokolow
Sound Engineer and Bass—Michael Monagan
Recorded at Sossity Sound

7777 W. BLUEMOUND RD. P.O. BOX 13819 MILWAUKEE, WI 53213
Publisher: Jim Beloff
Edited by Ronny S. Schiff
Cover and Art Direction by Elizabeth Maihock Beloff
Graphics and Music Typography by Charylu Roberts
Photograph of Fred Sokolow by E. K. Waller

Introduction

Okay, so Bill Monroe never had a ukulele player in his band, and neither did any other famous bluegrass band…yet. But why should that stop you from jamming with bluegrass players, strumming along with the tunes on your uke and, yes, playing fast-picked instrumental solos? This book will show you how to do all that. For each of the bluegrass favorites in this collection, you'll learn to…

- Strum the chords and sing the tune and…

- Play an instrumental solo, picking the melody and strumming to fill out the rhythm, and…

- Play a fingerpicking solo using banjo-type, three-finger rolls.

This is new, stylistically, for the uke, but bluegrass-style soloing fits the uke like a glove—as one listen to the audio will demonstrate. Like the 5-string banjo, the uke has a high string where the lowest one should be. As a result, fast, three-finger banjo rolls, which are one of the main musical features of bluegrass, translate well to ukulele.

So, boldly go where few *ukists* have gone before, and learn a whole new way of picking the uke, and a whole bunch of great bluegrass tunes!

Happy picking,

Fred Sokolow

www.sokolowmusic.com

P.S. The audio that comes with this book includes all the tunes (three arrangements of each), plus the exercises and rolls in the introductory chapters. It's always helpful to listen to each song, arrangement or exercise several times, before trying to learn it on the uke.

P.P.S. In addition to bluegrass banjo-style soloing, the uke can play fancy fingerpicking backup during vocals, and during solos by other instruments. You can see and hear this type of accompaniment on the tune "Take This Hammer."

Visit us on the web at **www.fleamarketmusic.com**

Three Picking Styles

There are three types of solos in this book:

- Strumming with the thumb picking the melody, much like Carter-style guitar.

- Strumming with the index finger picking the melody, like Pete Seeger's "basic strum" for 5-string banjo, or the banjo "clawhammer" style.

- Rolling a la Earl Scruggs' banjo rolls; the melody stands out amidst the fast, syncopated, three-finger rolls.

Here's an introduction to each of the three picking techniques:

Strumming, Thumb Lead

This technique resembles the "church lick" or "Carter lick" popularized by Maybelle Carter in the early 1930s, when she recorded with the Carter Family. Their records are the backbone of country music and, to some extent, bluegrass as well. Mother Maybelle's solos may be the first guitar solos on a country record, as most Southern string bands prior to the Carter Family used the guitar as a rhythm instrument. Her playing has been widely imitated and, to this day, it's considered the basic acoustic guitar soloing style in country music.

The Carter lick works best when most of the melody falls on the ukulele's 3rd (C) and 4th (G) strings. For example, look at the strumming arrangement for "Banks Of The Ohio" or "Old Joe Clark."

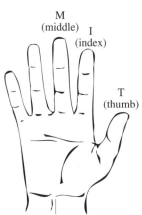

The basic strum has three movements:

- The thumb picks down on a single string.

- The index or middle finger (whichever feels more comfortable) brushes down on the 1st and 2nd strings (and the 3rd string if you're picking very energetically).

- The index or middle finger brushes up on the 1st and 2nd strings.

The resulting rhythmic strum has a "bump-ditty" feel:

TRACK 1

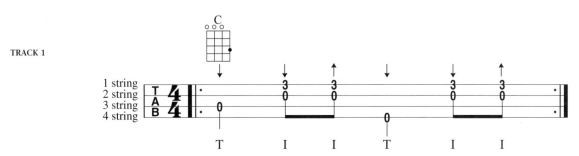

Often, to express the melody, the thumb will pick several single notes in a row, followed by the brush up and brush down:

TRACK 2

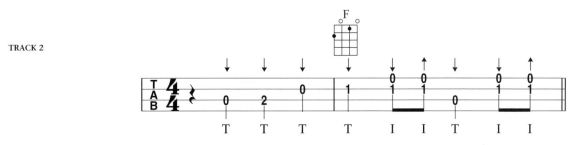

3

Strumming, Index Lead

Pete Seeger popularized this 5-string banjo technique and called it the "basic strum." It has the same "bump-ditty" rhythm as the Carter lick, but the index finger picks the melody notes instead of the thumb. Here's the basic pattern:

- The index finger picks up on a single string.

- The middle or ring finger (whichever feels more comfortable) brushes down on the 1st and 2nd strings (and the 3rd string if you're picking very energetically).

- The thumb picks the 4th (G) string.

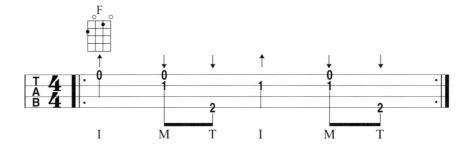

Often, the index finger will play a series of melody notes, followed by the brush down and thumb-picking-the-4th-string:

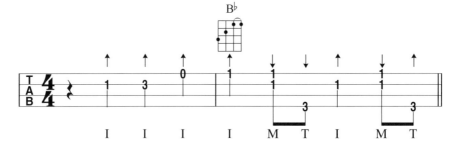

This technique works well on songs whose melody falls mainly on the 1st and 2nd strings. For example, see the strumming arrangements of "Boil Them Cabbage Down" and "Little Maggie."

The more traditional, "frailing" or "clawhammer" banjo style can be used as well. It's exactly like the basic strum, except the index finger picks *down*, instead of up, on a single string:

- The index finger picks down on a single string, using the fingernail.

- The index, middle or ring finger (whichever feels more comfortable) brushes down on the 1st and 2nd strings (and the 3rd string if you're picking very energetically).

- The thumb picks the 4th (G) string.

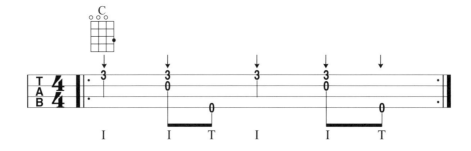

Clawhammer, which gets its name from the claw-like shape your picking hand assumes when playing this way, has a slightly more percussive sound than the Pete Seeger-style strum.

Rolling

Earl Scruggs perfected a banjo fingerpicking style based on thumb-and-two-finger-rolls (often referred to as "three-finger picking"). It works well on the ukulele, because the two instruments have in common the odd high-pitched string (the 4th string on the uke, 5th string on the banjo).

Here are some of the basic rolls. Practice each one by repeating it over and over, as heard on the recording, but realize that when you play a Scruggs-style solo, you mix up all the different rolls in all kinds of seemingly random sequences. The "rolling" arrangements that follow will show you how this is done.

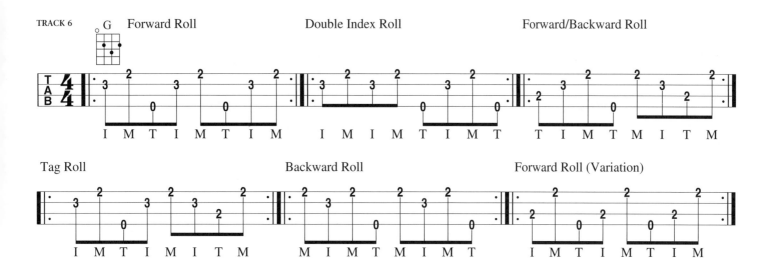

Fiddle Tunes

Although singing is important in bluegrass music, instrumental solos are also part of most bluegrassers' repertoires. Some of the most popular instrumentals are fiddle tunes, many of which are a hundred and fifty years old (or older). Often, they came from the British Isles and were given new names in America. Usually, players swap solos: the fiddle plays the tune one time around, the mandolin or banjo does the same thing, and now the uke will take a turn as well!

Most fiddle tunes have two sections—an A part (verse) and a B part (chorus)—and in the typical fiddle tune, you play each part twice in a row. Once around the tune, then, is AABB (two verses followed by two choruses).

Although any song can be played in any key, the old fiddle tunes have "traditional" keys that most pickers use. "Sally Goodin" is almost always played in A, "Soldier's Joy" in D, and so on. These key choices were largely influenced by the ease in which the tunes can be played on the fiddle; A and D are the easiest keys for a standard-tuned fiddle. Even though these may not be the easiest keys on the uke, it's best to learn the fiddle tunes in their traditional keys, as that's how most folks play them in jam sessions and performances.

Many fiddle tunes, including the ones in this book, have lyrics, but bluegrassers usually play them as instrumentals. Just for fun, we've included lyrics to some of the fiddle tunes in this collection.

Many of the songs in this collection are well over a century old. If the lyrics occasionally differ from those used by contemporary bluegrass groups, it's because they are taken from very old (closer to the original) versions of the songs.

Banks Of The Ohio

TRACK 7

Like other murder ballads ("Pretty Polly," "Little Sadie," "Omie Wise,") "Banks of the Ohio" is at least a century old and of uncertain origin. It has been recorded ever since the art of recording began and is a staple among bluegrass bands.

Traditional

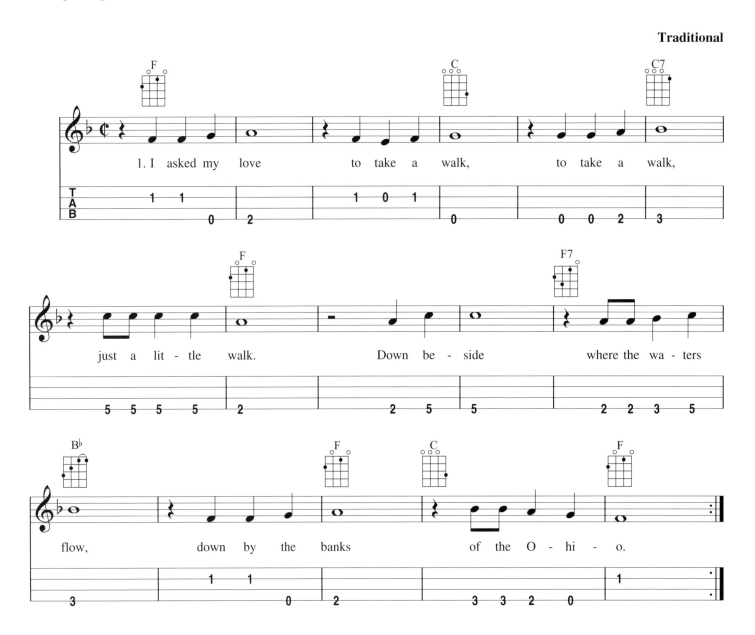

Additional Lyrics

Chorus:
Then only say that you'll be mine, in no other arms entwine.
Down beside where waters flow, down by the banks of the Ohio.

Additional Verses:

2. I took her by her lily-white hand and led her down where the waters stand.
   There I pushed her in to drown, and I watched her as she floated down.

3. I started home 'tween twelve and one, I cried "My God, what have I done?
   I killed the only woman I loved, because she would not marry me."

Strumming (thumb lead):

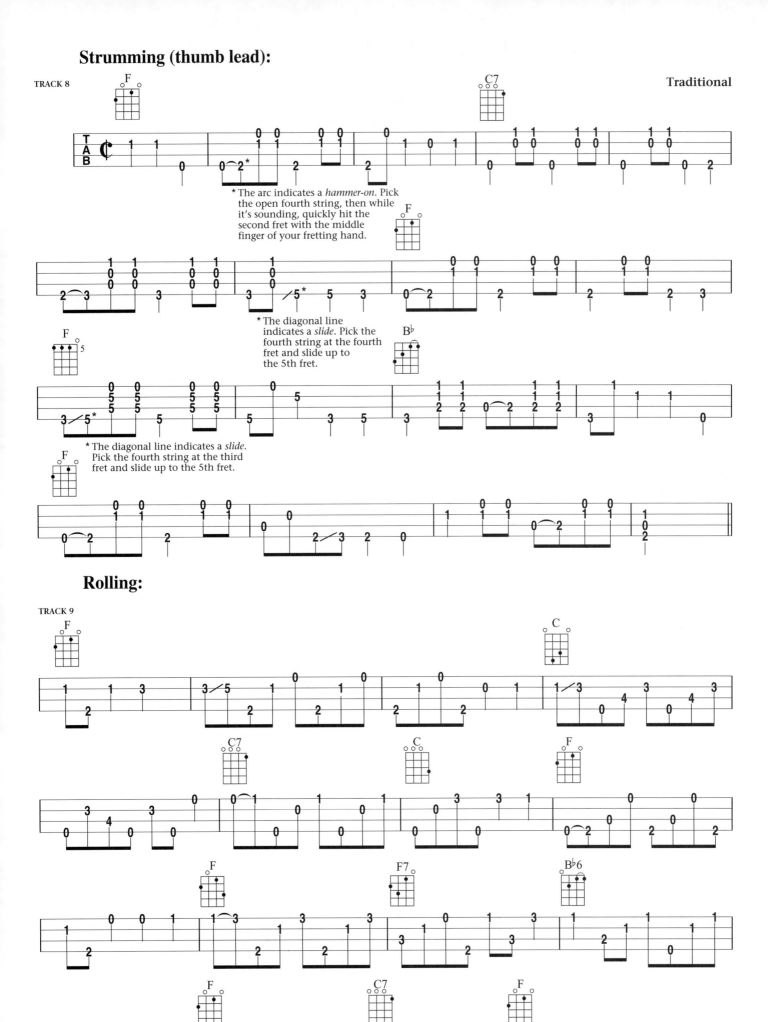

* The arc indicates a *hammer-on*. Pick the open fourth string, then while it's sounding, quickly hit the second fret with the middle finger of your fretting hand.

* The diagonal line indicates a *slide*. Pick the fourth string at the fourth fret and slide up to the 5th fret.

* The diagonal line indicates a *slide*. Pick the fourth string at the third fret and slide up to the 5th fret.

Rolling:

Boil Them Cabbage Down

TRACK 10

This is one of the first tunes beginning fiddlers learn, as it's very easy to play in the key of A on the violin. Maybe that's one reason it's so popular! There are many lyrics, but most bluegrassers play it as an instrumental.

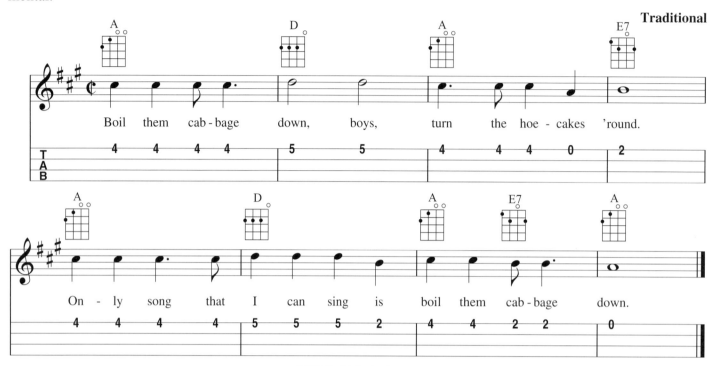

Strumming (index lead):

TRACK 11

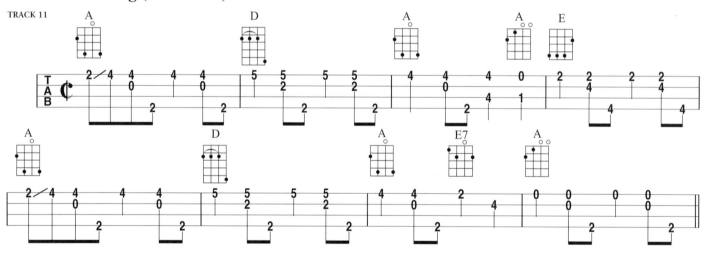

Rolling:

TRACK 12

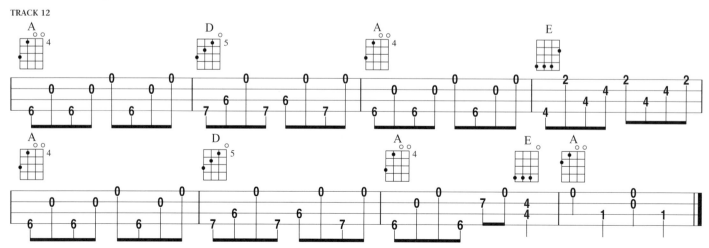

8

Bury Me Beneath The Willow

TRACK 13

This old parlor song was the first tune the Carter Family recorded during their historic first recording session in Bristol, Tennessee, in 1927. Sara and Maybelle Carter said they had known it since childhood. It has become a bluegrass standard.

Traditional

Additional Lyrics

3. They told me that she did not love me, I could not believe it's true,
   until an angel softly whispered she no longer cares for you.

4. Tomorrow was to be our wedding. Lord, oh Lord where can she be?
   She's gone, she's gone to find another. She no longer cares for me.

Strumming (index lead):

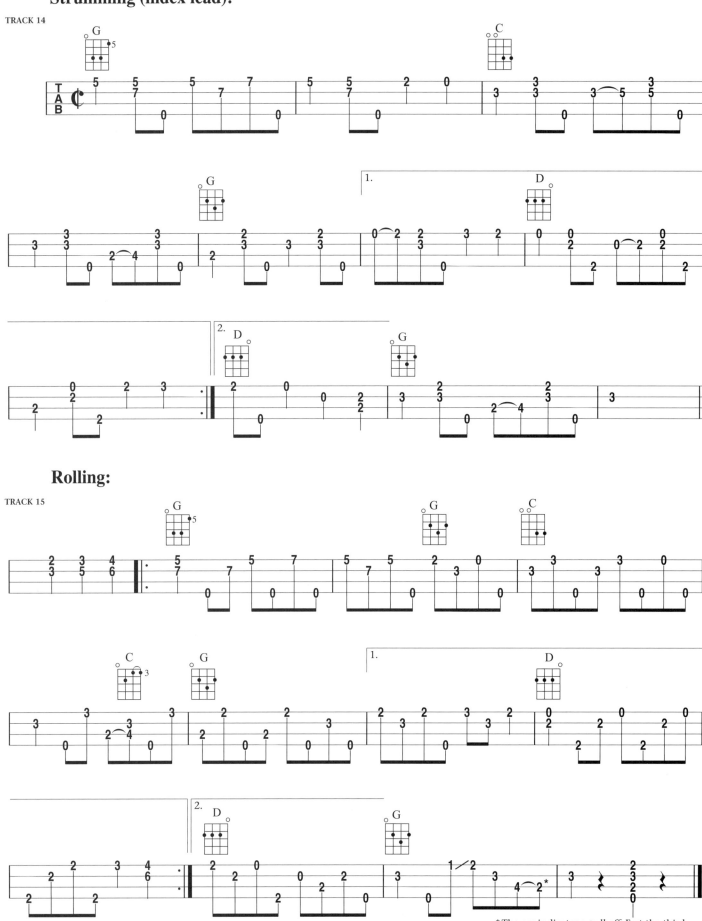

Rolling:

*The arc indicates a *pull-off*. Fret the third string at the second fret with your index finger *and* at the fourth fret with your little finger. Pick the string at the fourth fret and, while it's still ringing, pluck down with the little finger of your fretting hand, sounding the note at the second fret.

Careless Love

Jazz, blues, rock, country, bluegrass and folk singers have been performing and recording versions of "Careless Love" for at least a century. Buddy Bolden, one of the originators of jazz, was among the first to popularize the tune. It is a lament by a girl whose man tired of her, after he got her pregnant.

Traditional

Additional Lyrics

2. Now my apron strings don't pin.
   Now my apron strings don't pin.
   Now my apron strings don't pin.
   You pass my door and you don't come in.

2. Cried last night and the night before.
   I cried last night and the night before.
   I cried last night and the night before.
   Gonna cry tonight and cry no more.

Strumming (index lead):

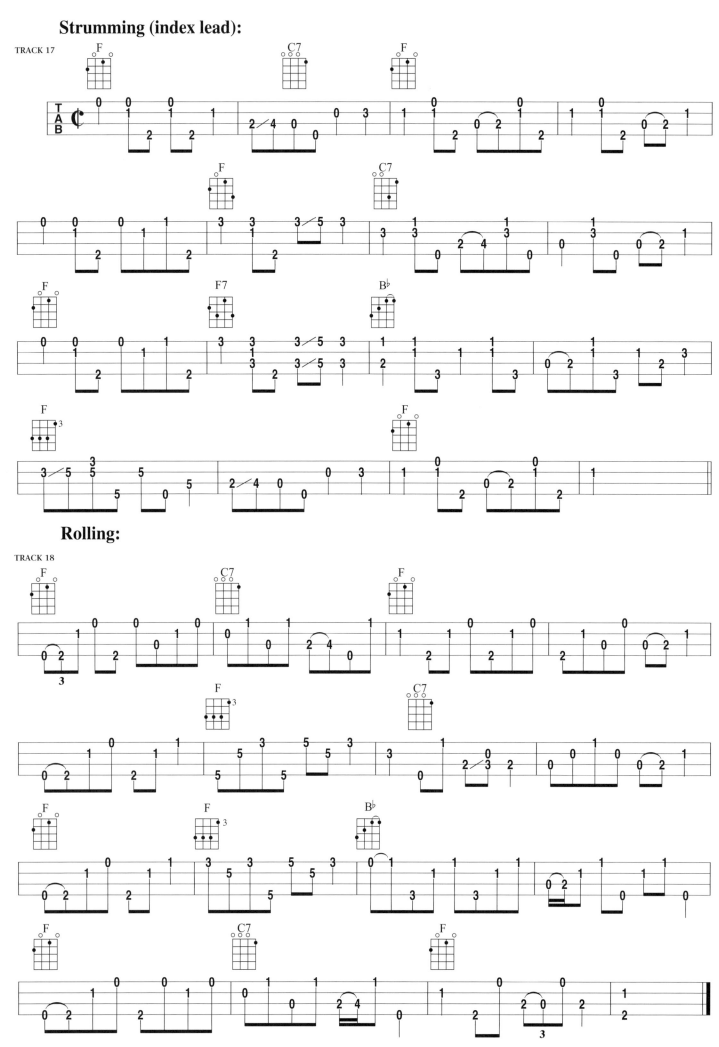

Rolling:

Come All Ye Fair And Tender Maidens

TRACK 19

This sad ballad of faded love shares some verses with its cousin, "The Water Is Wide." It probably comes from the British Isles and crossed the ocean to be transformed in Appalachia. Bluegrassers usually sing "Come all you fair and tender ladies."

Traditional

1. Come all ye fair and ten-der maid-ens, take warn-ing how you court young men. They're like a star of a sum-mer morn-ing. They'll first ap-pear, and then they're gone.

Additional Lyrics

2. They'll tell to you such lovely stories, and make you think that they love you well,
   and away they'll go and court some other, and leave you there in grief to dwell.

3. I wish I was a little sparrow and I had wings to fly so high.
   I'd fly to the arms of my false true lover, and when he'd ask, I would deny.

4. Oh, love is handsome, love is charming, and love is pretty while it's new.
   But love grows cold as love grows older, and fades away like the morning dew.

Strumming (thumb lead):

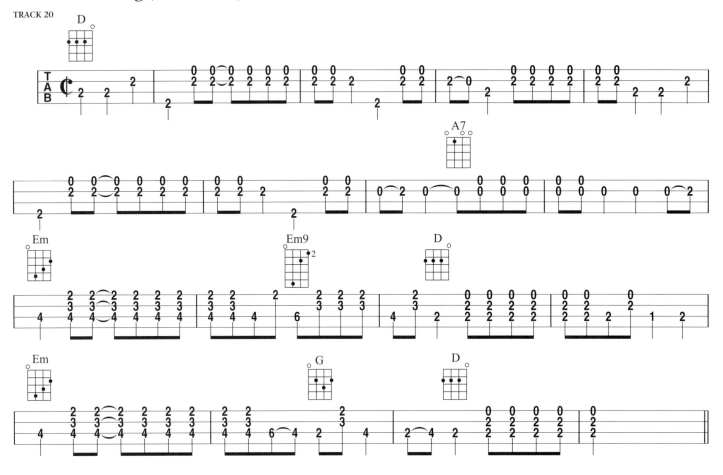

Rolling:

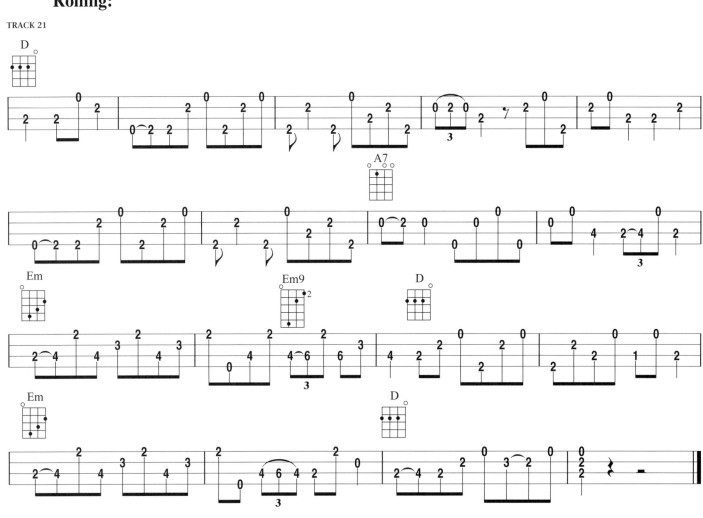

14

Goin' Down The Road Feeling Bad

Also known as "Lonesome Road Blues," this tune has been performed and recorded by white and African American performers as long as phonograph recordings have existed. Earl Scruggs and other bluegrassers have played it as an instrumental. It's in the Grateful Dead repertoire (along with many other traditional folk and blues tunes).

Traditional

Additional Lyrics

2. I'm down in the jailhouse on my knees. Down in the jailhouse on my knees.
   Down in the jailhouse on my knees, Lord, Lord. I ain't gonna be treated this a-way.

3. They feed me on corn bread and beans. They feed me on corn bread and beans .
   They feed me on corn bread and beans, Lord, Lord. I ain't gonna be treated this a-way.

4. Two dollar shoes hurt my feet, two dollar shoes hurt my feet.
   Two dollar shoes hurt my feet, Lord, Lord. I ain't gonna be treated this a-way.

5. I'm going where the climate suits my clothes, I'm going where the climate suits my clothes.
   Going where the climate suits my clothes, Lord, Lord. I ain't gonna be treated this a-way

Strumming (index lead):

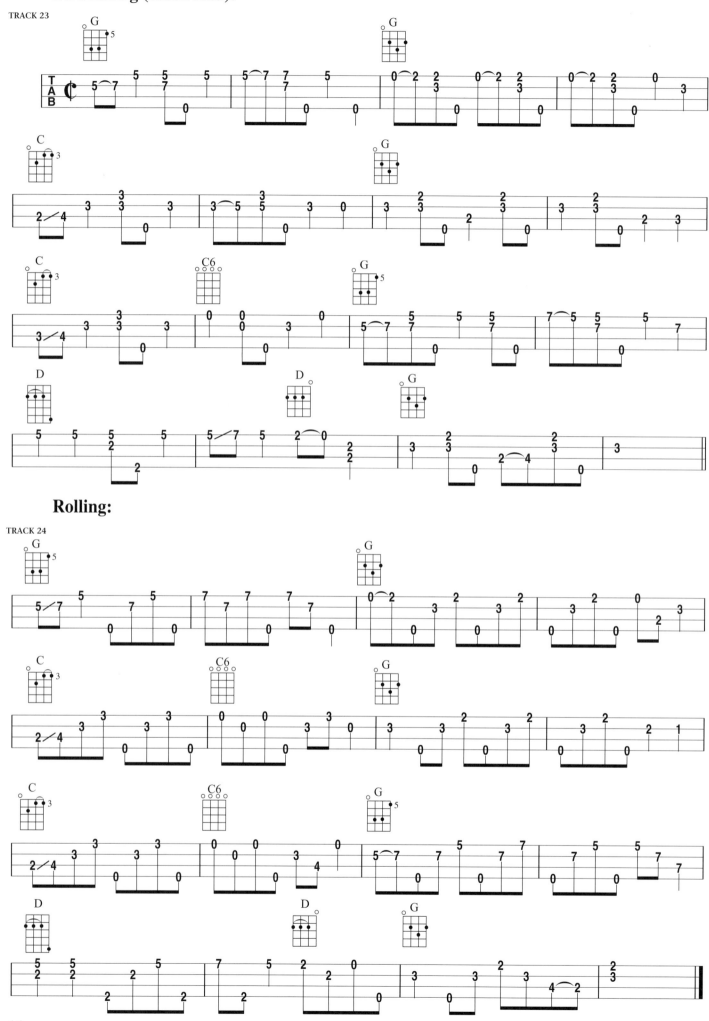

Rolling:

16

John Hardy

For over a century, folks have been singing about John Hardy, an African American steel-driver, like John Henry. Hardy was hung in 1894 for shooting and killing a man in an argument over a card game. It is sung by some, played as an instrumental by others.

Additional Lyrics

2. John Hardy, he got to the Keystone Bridge,
he thought that he would be free.
And up stepped a man and took him by his arm, says
"Johnny, walk along with me,
Johnny walk along with me."

3. He sent for his papa and his mama too,
to come and go his bail.
But money won't buy a murdering case.
They locked John Hardy back in jail,
locked John Hardy back in jail.

4. John Hardy had a pretty little girl,
the dress she wore was blue.
And she came skipping through the old jail hall, saying,
"Papa, I've been true to you,
Papa I've been true to you."

5. I been to the East and I been to the West,
I been this wide world around.
I been to the river and I been baptized,
and now I'm on my hanging ground.
Now I'm on my hanging ground.

Strumming (index lead):

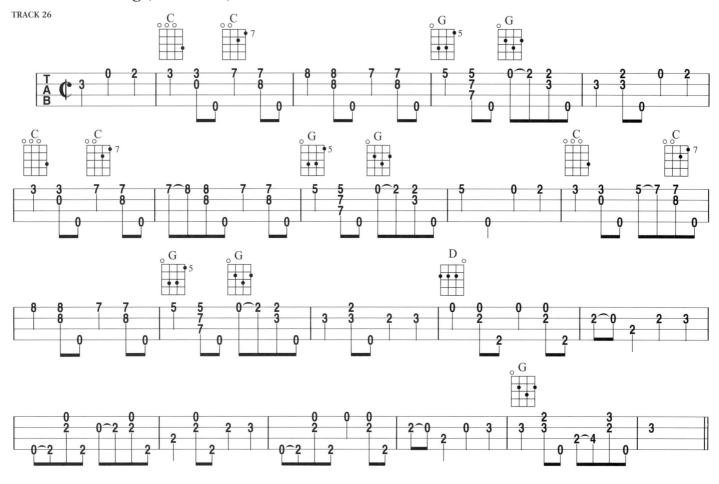

Rolling:

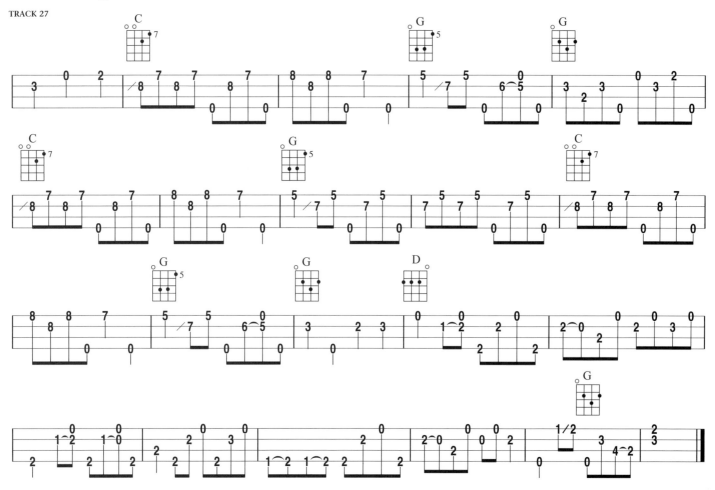

John Henry

TRACK 28

There probably was a steel-driving African American named John Henry who lost his contest with a steam drill around 1873, working in the Big Bend tunnel on the C & O line in West Virginia. He drove drills into rock to make holes for blasting charges. But his story has become a parable about man versus machine, and many of the details are embroidery and myth. Bill Monroe and other bluegrassers have sung versions of it, and Earl Scruggs and many more soloists have played it as an instrumental.

Traditional

Additional Lyrics

2. The captain said to John Henry, "I'm gonna bring that steam drill around.
I'm gonna bring that steam drill out on the job,
I'm gonna whup that steel on down, Lord, Lord, whup that steel on down."

3. John Henry told his captain "A man ain't nothing but a man,
   but before I let your steam drill beat me down,
   I'll die with a hammer in my hand, Lord, Lord, die with a hammer in my hand."

4. John Henry said to his shaker, "Shaker why don't you pray?
   'Cause if I miss this little piece of steel,
   tomorrow be your burying day, Lord, Lord, tomorrow be your burying day."

5. John Henry hammered in the mountains. His hammer was striking fire,
   and the last words I hear that poor boy say,
   "Gimme a cold drink of water 'fore I die, Lord, Lord, cool drink of water 'fore I die."

6. John Henry, he drove fifteen feet, steam drill only made nine.
   But he drove so hard that he broke his poor heart,
   and he laid down his hammer and he died, Lord, Lord, laid down his hammer and he died.

7. So every Monday morning when the bluebirds begin to sing,
   you can see John Henry out on the line.
   You can hear John Henry's hammer ring, Lord, Lord, hear John Henry's hammer ring.

Strumming (index lead):

TRACK 29

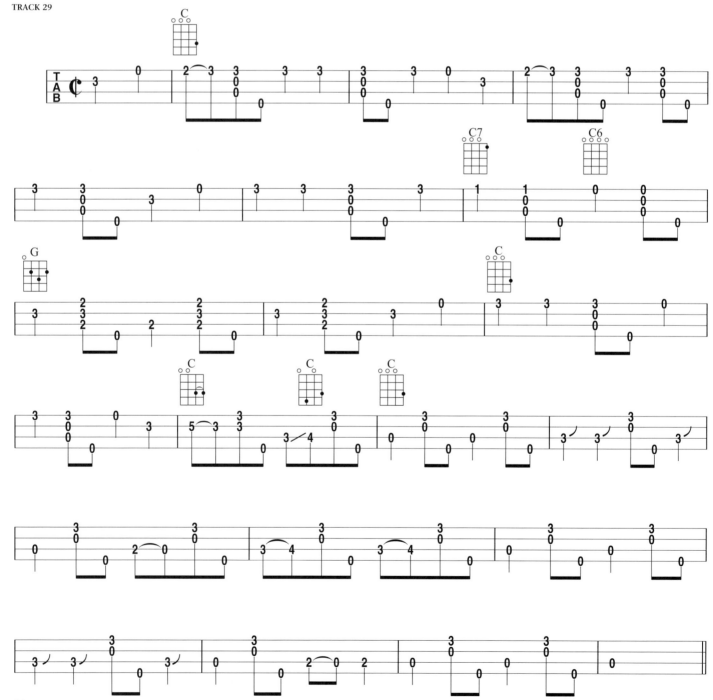

Rolling:

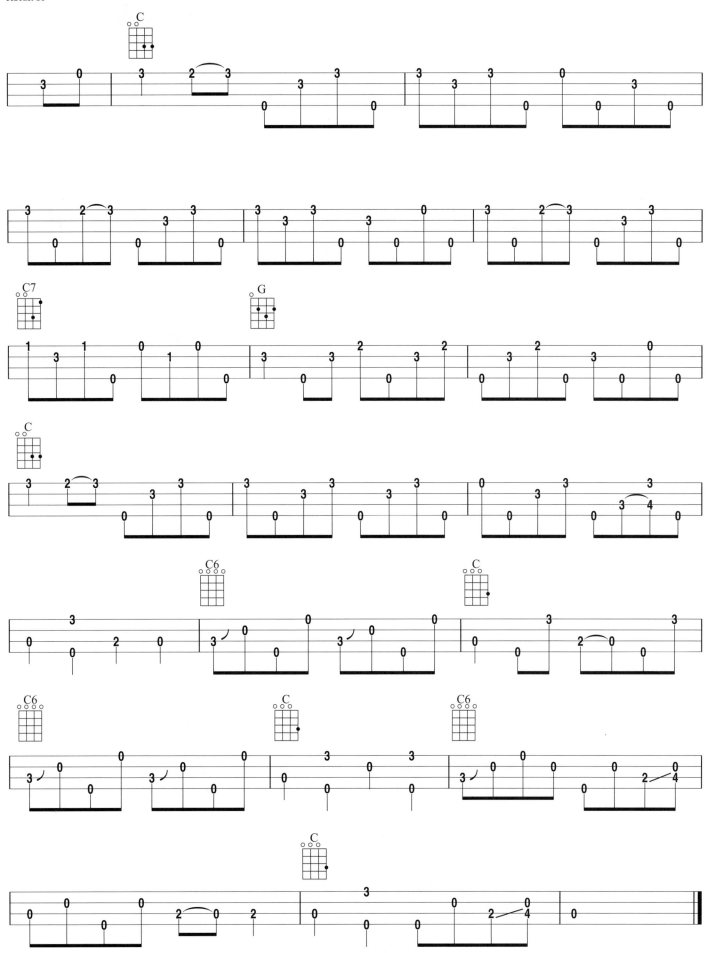

Little Maggie

Like "Darling Cory," Little Maggie is the archetypal outlaw woman, popularized by many bluegrass songs. In most of the tunes she has a gun, a bottle of whiskey and a banjo…a dangerous combination!

Traditional

Additional Lyrics

2. How could I ever stand it to see those two blue eyes?
   They shine just like the diamonds, like the diamonds in the skies.

3. Last time I saw little Maggie, she was sittin' on the banks of the sea
   with a forty-four strapped around her and a banjo on her knee.

4. Pretty flowers were made for bloomin', pretty stars were made to shine.
   Pretty women were made for lovin'. Little Maggie was made to be mine.

5. I'm goin' down to the station with a suitcase in my hand.
   I'm goin' away for to leave you, goin' to some far distant land.

6. Go away, go away, little Maggie, go and do the best you can.
   I'll get me another woman; you can get you another man.

Strumming (index lead):

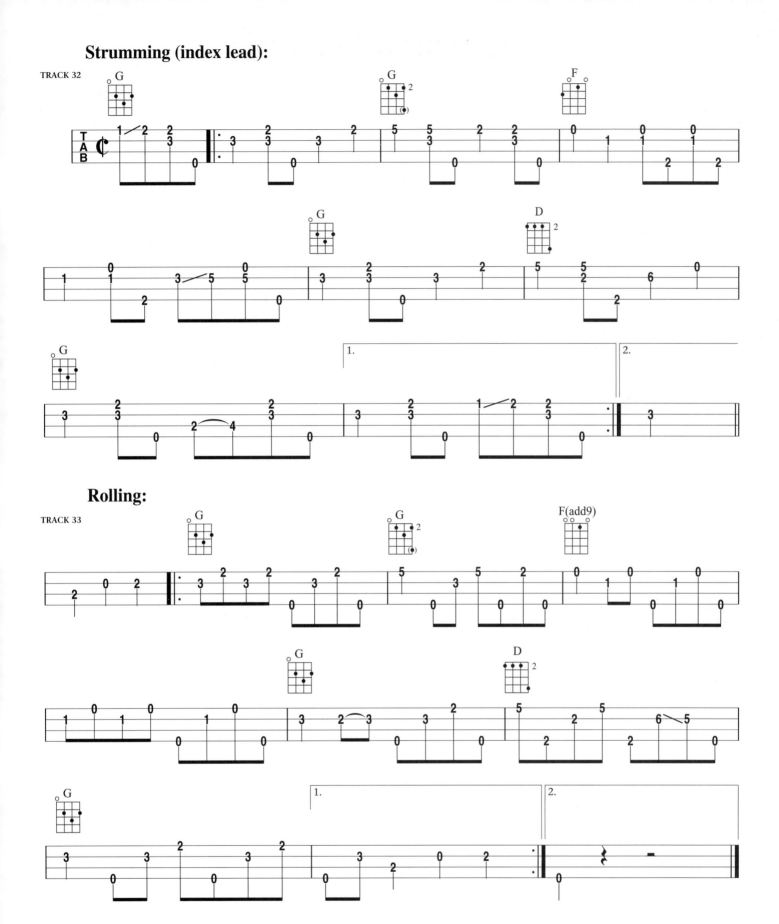

Rolling:

Nine Pound Hammer

TRACK 34

In the work song tradition (see "Take This Hammer"), "Nine Pound Hammer" was popular among string bands in the 1920s and '30s, and was later associated with Merle Travis.

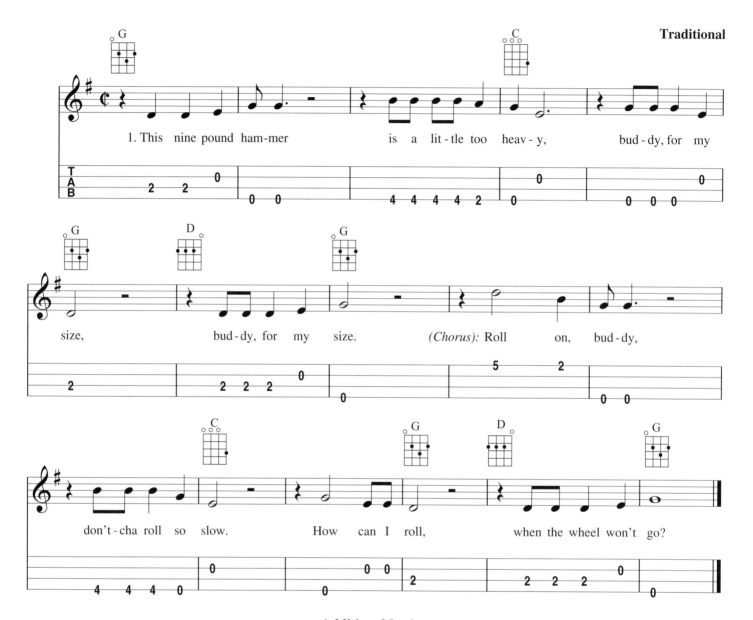

Traditional

Additional Lyrics

2. I'm going on the mountain, for to see my baby,
   and I ain't coming back, no I ain't coming back.

3. There ain't no hammer, down in this tunnel
   that can ring like mine, that can ring like mine.

4. Rings like silver, and it shines like gold.
   Rings like silver, and it shines like gold.

5. This old hammer, it killed John Henry.
   Ain't gonna kill me, it ain't gonna kill me.

6. It's a long way to Harlan, and a long way to Hazard
   just to get a little brew, just to get a little brew.

Strumming (thumb lead):

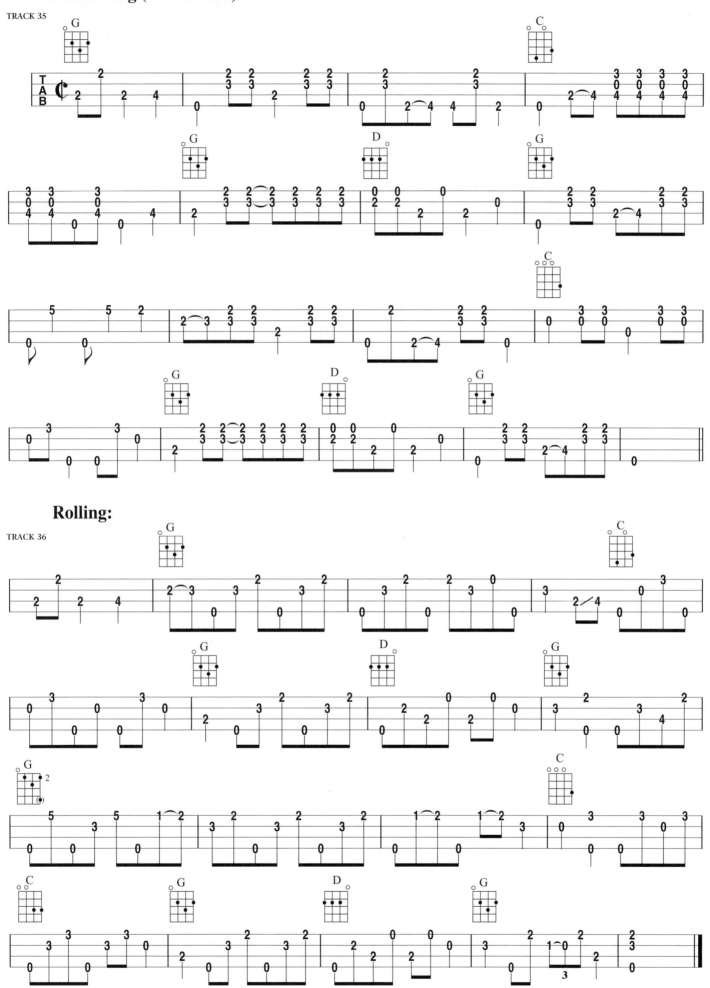

Rolling:

Old Joe Clark

TRACK 37

In 1970, the Kentucky historical society put up a monument (outside a post office) to "Old Joe Clark Ballad." It says the song was printed in 1918 and that it concerns Joe Clark, a Kentucky mountaineer who ran a government-supervised still and was murdered in 1885. His place of burial and many details of his life are well documented. But there are several other Joe Clark stories involving different locales, including a Maryland murder of Herbert Brown committed by Clark and Herbert's wife Betsy, who appears in the lyrics to many versions of the tune.

Whoever he was, the song named after him is one of the most often-played fiddle tunes anywhere old time music or bluegrass are heard. Despite the ninety-plus verses that appear in various songbooks, "Old Joe Clark" is usually played as an instrumental. Here's a sample verse: "I would not marry an old school-teacher, tell you the reason why: She'd blow her nose in old cornbread and call it pumpkin pie."

Traditional

Strumming (thumb lead):

TRACK 38

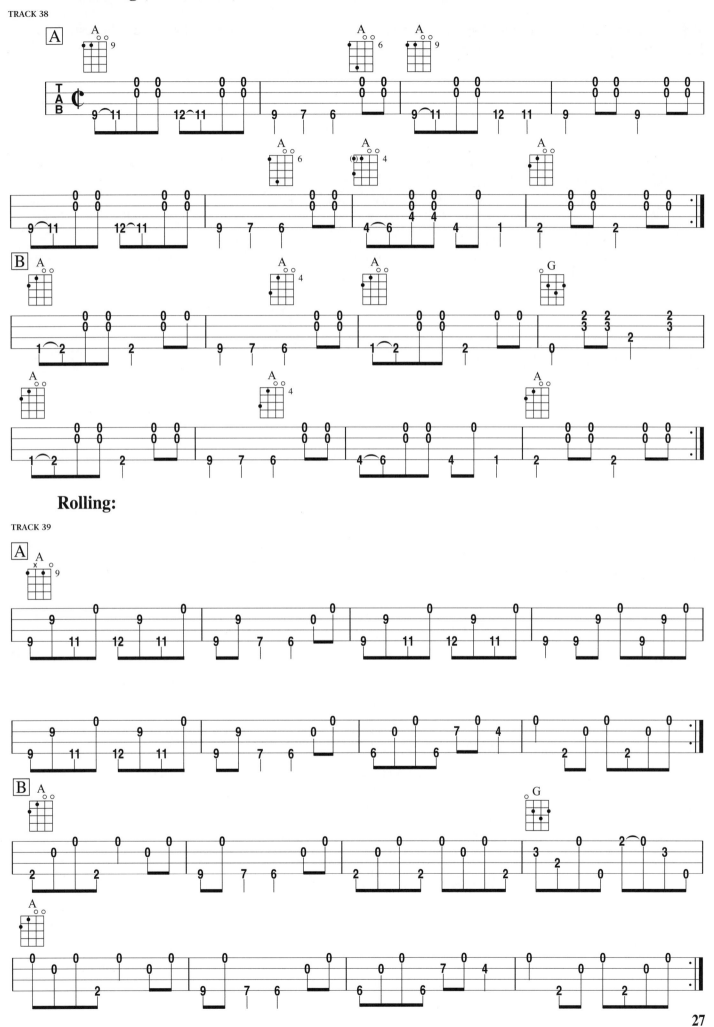

Rolling:

TRACK 39

27

Roll In My Sweet Baby's Arms

Bill and Charlie Monroe recorded an early version of this traditional tune in the 1930s, and countless bluegrass and country artists have recorded it since then.

Traditional

1. Ain't gon - na work on the rail - road. Ain't gon - na
Chorus: Roll in my sweet ba - by's arms,___ roll in my

work on the farm.
sweet ba - by's arms.
Gon - na lay 'round the shack 'til the

mail train comes back and I'll roll in my sweet ba - by's arms.

Additional Verses

2. Now where was you last Friday night while I was lyin' in jail?
   Walkin' the streets with another man, you wouldn't even go my bail.

3. I know your parents don't like me, they drove me away from your door.
   If I had my life to live over again, I'd never go there anymore.

4. Mama's a beauty operator, sister can weave and can spin.
   Dad's got an interest in the old cotton mill, just watch the money roll in.

Strumming (thumb lead):

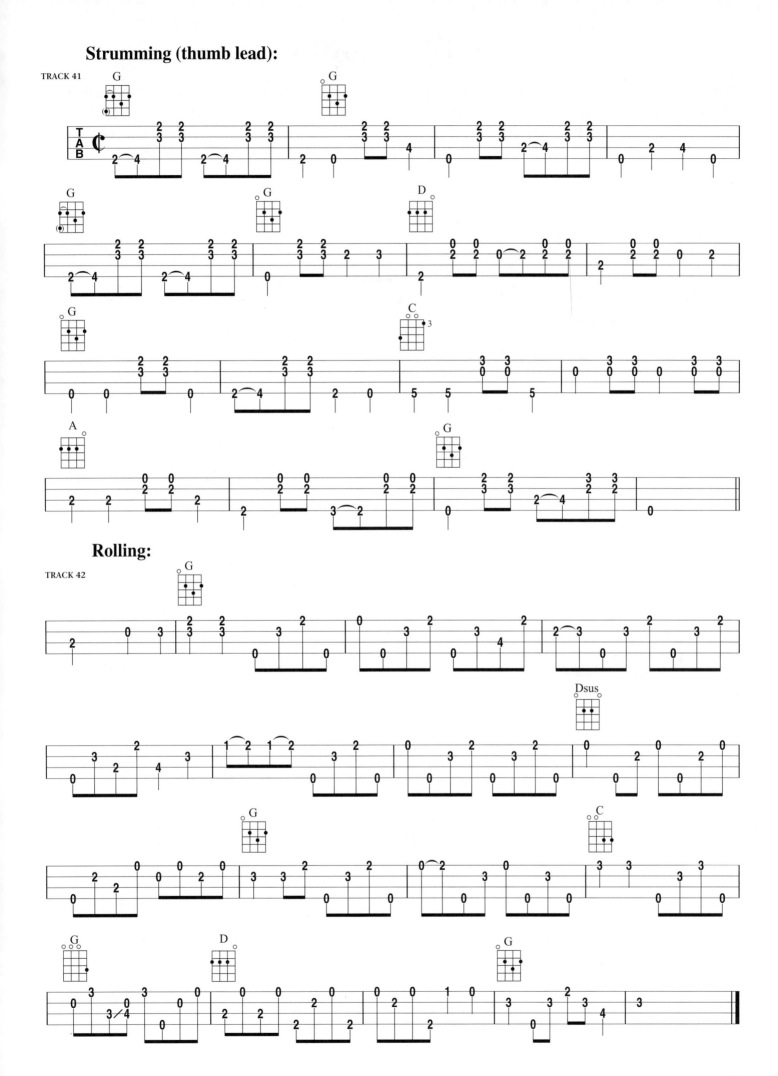

Rolling:

Sally Goodin

TRACK 43

Texas fiddler Eck Robertson's recording of "Sally Goodin" was the number one country music bestseller of 1923. The song probably goes back a century before that, and it has been on Southern fiddlers' A-list as long as anyone can remember. Paul McCartney referred to it and played a few bars in his song, "Sally G." There is a lot of folklore about a woman called Sally Goodin who ran a boarding house in Civil War times, another gal who encouraged a fiddling contest between two suitors (one was Mr. Goodin) and so on. The true story is lost in antiquity!

Traditional

Strumming (index lead):

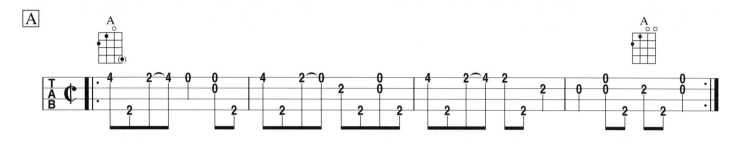

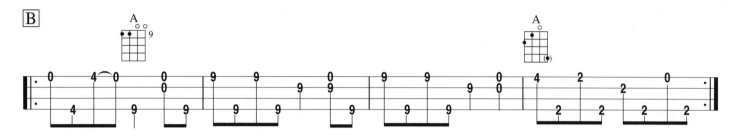

Rolling:

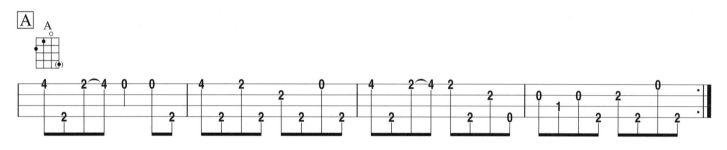

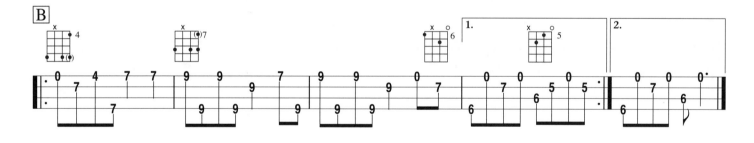

Soldier's Joy

TRACK 46

"Soldiers' Joy" was already printed in numerous sheet music and dance instruction manuals in the late 1700s in the British Isles and America. It has become one of the most popular fiddle tunes of all time, and many lyricists have had a go at it. There's some debate about what gave the soldiers joy: morphine, liquor and coming home from war have all been suggested in various lyrics. These days, the song is seldom sung and often played.

Traditional

Strumming (index lead):

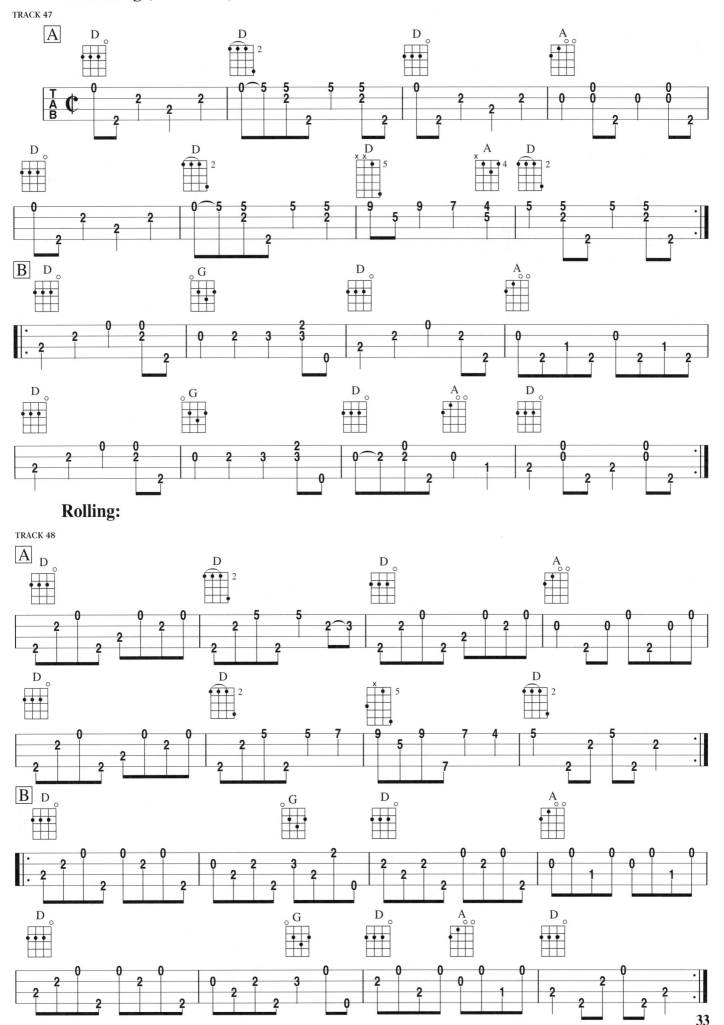

Rolling:

33

Take This Hammer

This southern work song was originally sung by shackled prisoners as they were breaking rocks. Singing established a rhythm the workers could endure, and the meter of the song has a breather, a pause, in which the hammer could be swung: "Take this hammer (whap!), carry it to the captain. (Whap!)" Flatt and Scruggs recorded a bluegrass version in the early 1960s, and countless bluegrass bands have sung it. The recording of "Take This Hammer" (track #51) includes a full bluegrass band, with the uke taking the place of the banjo. Some of the uke's fancy backup (accompaniment that is played during the singing) is tabbed out, below, and there are some remarks about it on the recording.

Additional Lyrics

2. If he asks you, was I running, if he asks you, was I running,
   if he asks you, was I running? Tell him I was flying, tell him I was flying.

3. If he asks you was I laughing, if he asks you was I laughing,
   if he asks you was I laughing? Tell him I was crying, tell him I was crying.

4. I don't want your cold iron shackles, I don't want your cold iron shackles,
   I don't want your cold iron shackles, it hurts my leg, it hurts my leg.

Strumming (index lead):

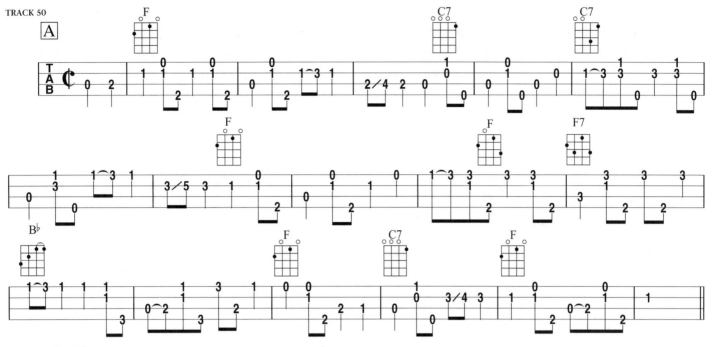

Rolling:

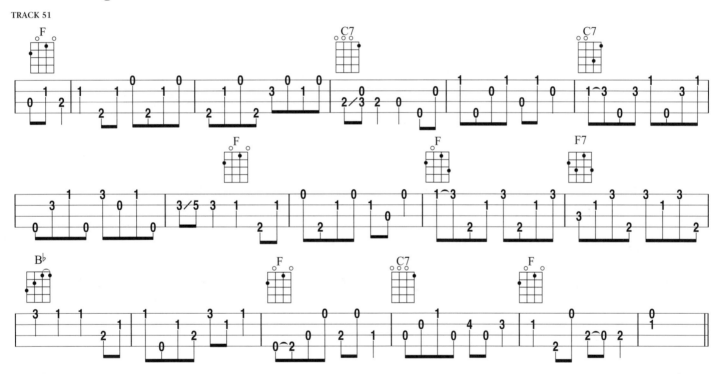

Backup:

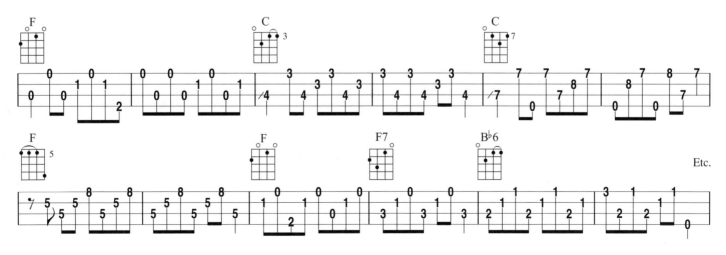

Etc.

Turkey In The Straw

The melody of this old fiddle tune has been sung with many lyrics, often comic ones. Many trace it back to a racist "coon" song called "The Old Zip Coon." It was already popular in the 1820s when blackface performers sang it, and since then it has been in wide use, appearing (usually as an instrumental) in some of the earliest cartoons, on children's recordings, on ice cream trucks and video games. Bluegrass bands usually play it as a fast instrumental. Note: in this and other fiddle tunes, the original melody is compromised ever so slightly (a note or two is changed here and there) because of the limitations of the ukulele. If the melody goes below the uke's lowest note (C), some original thinking is required!

Traditional

Strumming (index lead):

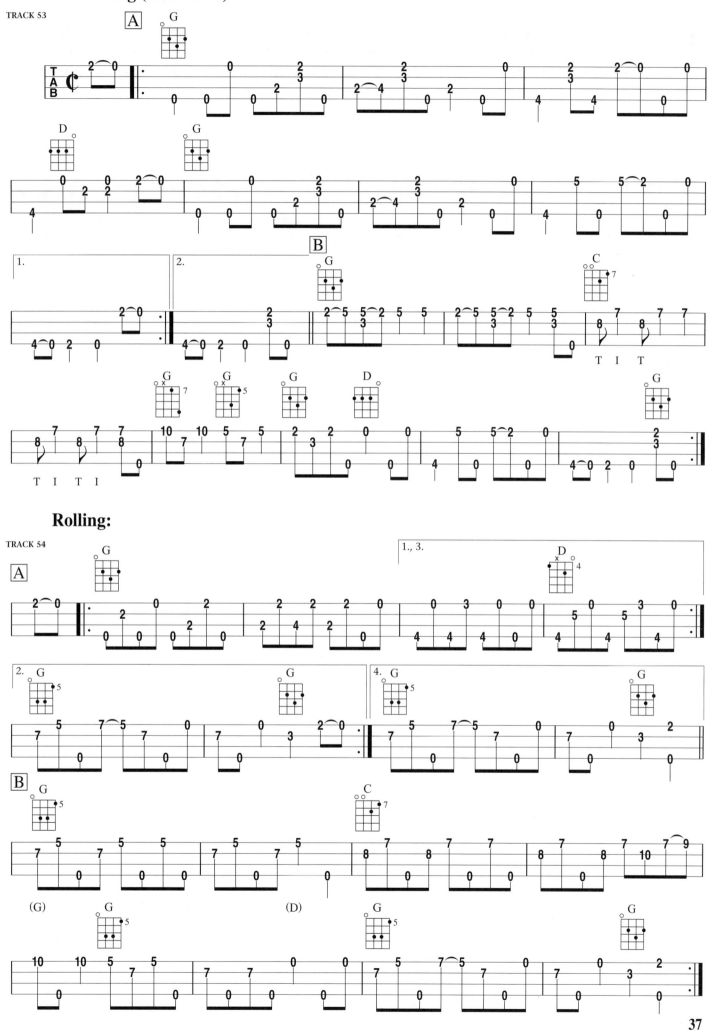

Rolling:

The Wabash Cannon Ball

TRACK 55

This is one of the most popular train songs. Two of the more memorable versions are the Carter Family's recording in 1929 and Roy Acuff's 1936 version. Both the train and Daddy Claxton may be fictitious, an invention, (The Carters sang about "Daddy Cleaton," and Roy Acuff's middle name was Claxton) but they have become legend.

Additional Lyrics

3. Oh, the Eastern states are dandy so the Western people say,
   from New York to St. Louis and Chicago by the way.
   Through the hills of Minnesota where the rippling waters fall,
   no chances can be taken on the Wabash Cannon Ball.

4. Here's to Daddy Claxton, may his name forever stand,
   and may he be remembered in the courts throughout our land.
   When his earthly race is over and the curtain around him falls,
   they'll carry him to glory on the Wabash Cannon Ball.

Strumming (index lead):

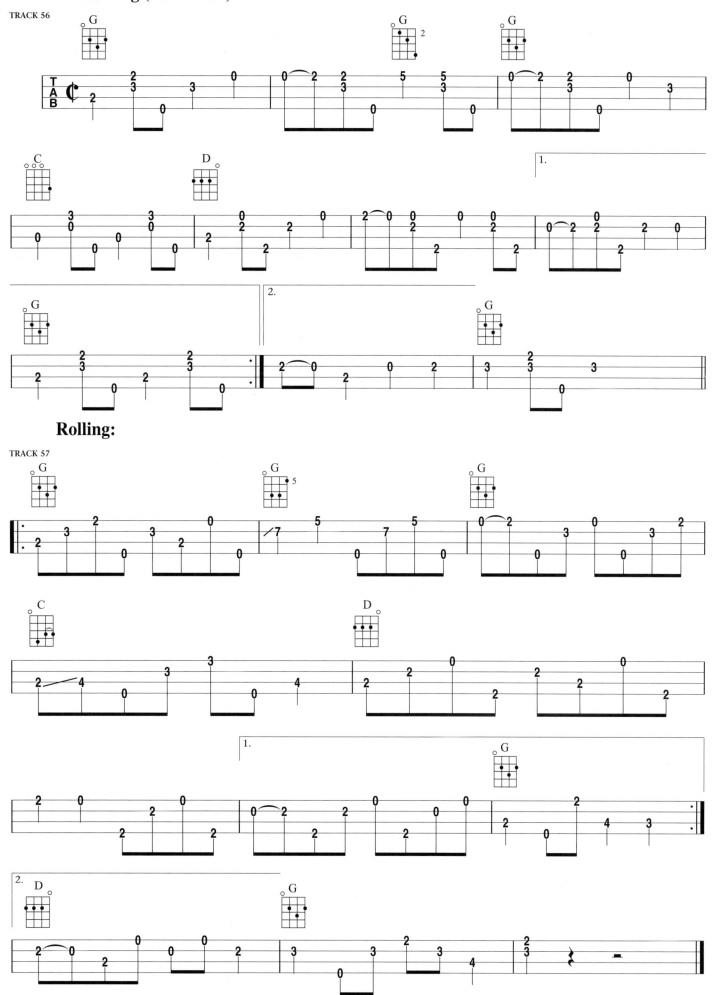

Rolling:

Wayfaring Stranger

The origins of this old spiritual are uncertain, and, like most of the songs in this book, the list of artists who have recorded it is long and diverse. In the early 1940s, it was folk singer Burl Ives' theme song on his radio show.

Traditional

Additional Lyrics

2. I know dark clouds will gather 'round me; I know my way is rough and steep.
   But beautiful fields lie just beyond me, where souls redeemed their vigil keep.
   I'm going there to meet my mother, she said she'd meet me when I come.
   I'm just a-going over Jordan, I'm only going over home.

Strumming (index lead):

TRACK 59

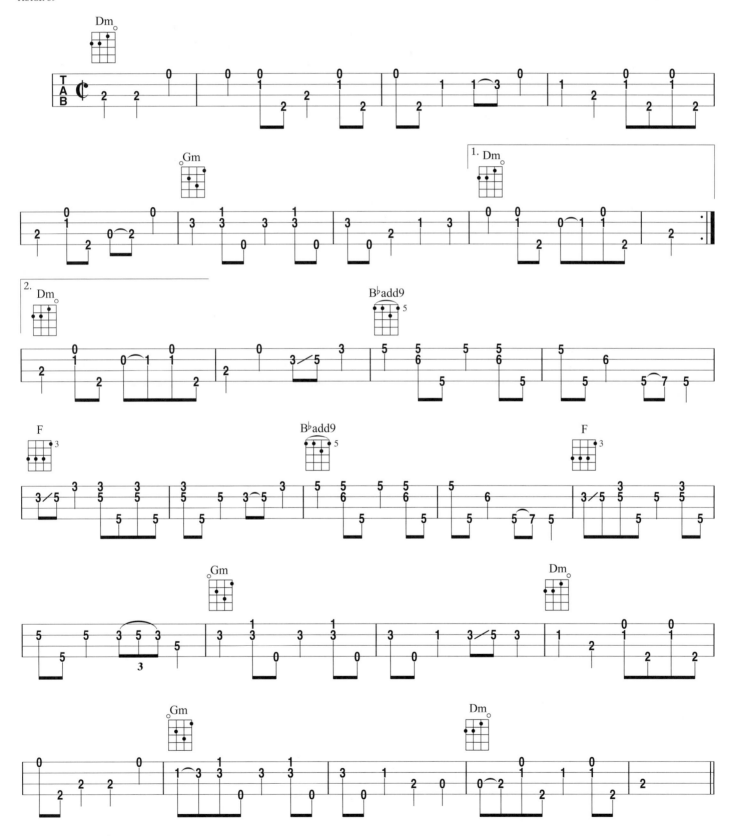

Rolling:

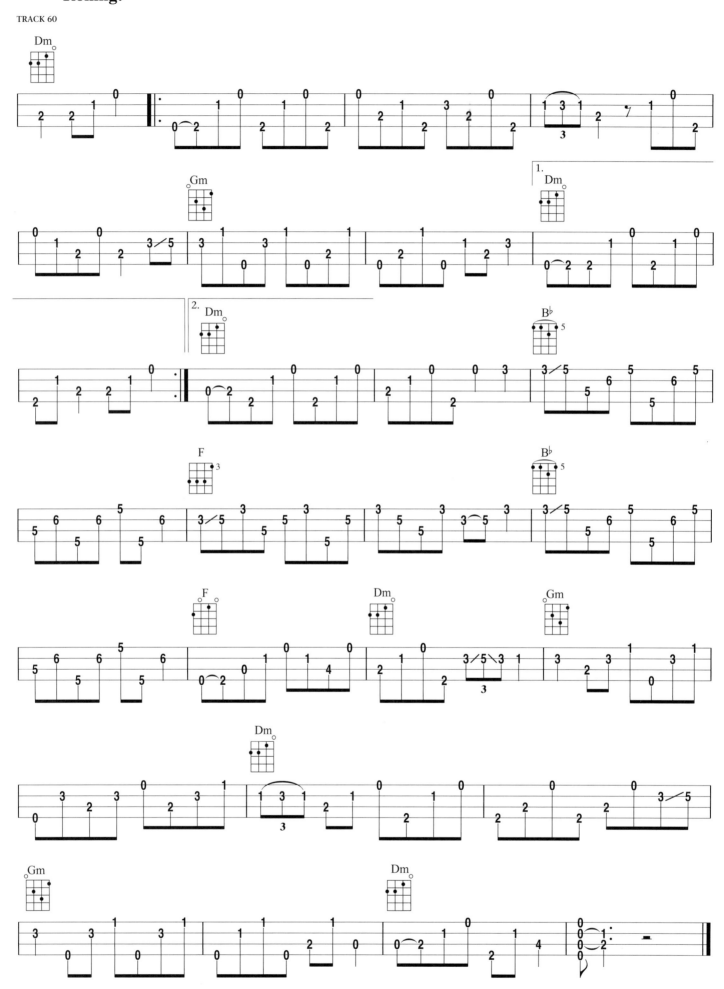

Wildwood Flower

TRACK 61

Inspired by one or possibly two nineteenth century parlor songs, "Wildwood Flower" became Maybelle Carter's signature song, and for decades it was considered a rite of passage for an acoustic guitarist to learn how to pick the tune as an instrumental.

Traditional

1. Oh, I'll twine 'mid the ring-lets of my ra-ven black hair,
with the lil-ies so pale and the ro-ses so fair,
and the myr-tle so bright with an em-er-ald hue,
and the pale dais-y with eyes of bright blue. 2. He

Additional Lyrics

2. He told me he loved me and promised to love,
through ill and misfortune all others above.
Another has won him, ah misery to tell.
He left me in silence with no word of farewell.

3. I'll dance, I'll sing and my laugh shall be gay.
I'll charm ev'ry heart, in this crowd I survey.
And I'll long to see him regret the dark hour
when he'd gone and neglected this pale wildwood flower.

Strumming (index lead):

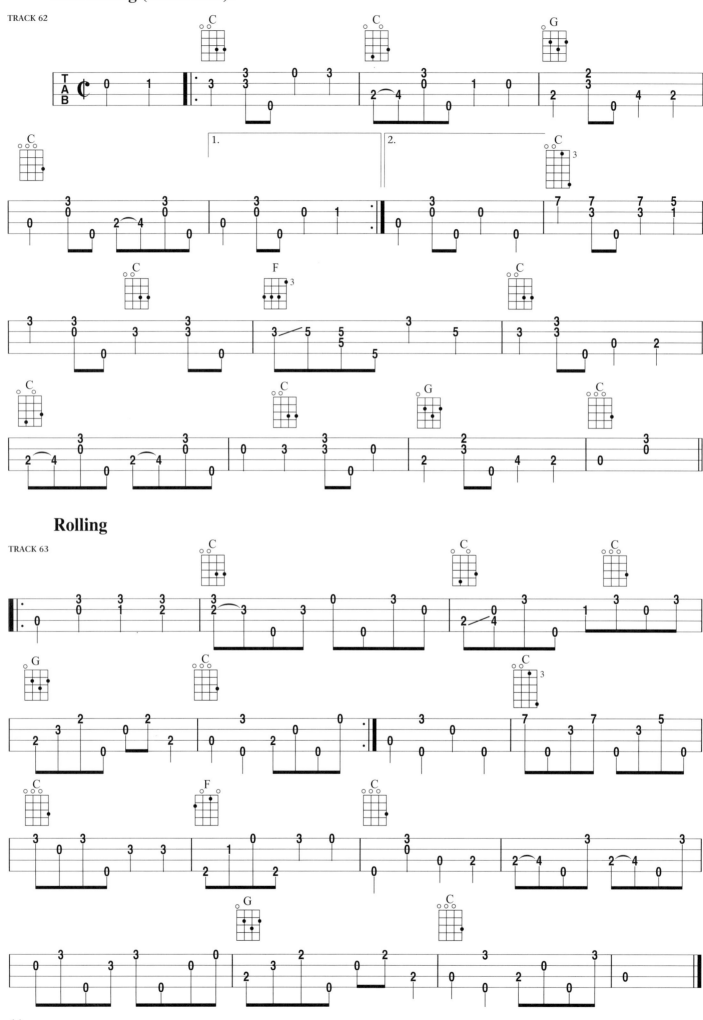

Rolling

44

Will The Circle Be Unbroken

Popularized by the Carter family, this tune has become a kind of anthem, often sung at the end of a bluegrass or country show. The early 1970's Nitty Gritty Dirt Band album, called *Will the Circle Be Unbroken*, is a good introduction to country and bluegrass music, as the band's guests read like a who's who of Opry and bluegrass stars.

Traditional

Additional Lyrics

2. Lord, I told the undertaker, "Undertaker, please drive slow,
   for this body you are hauling, Lord, I hate to see her go."

3. I followed close behind her, tried to hold up and be brave.
   But I could not hide my sorrow when they laid her in the grave.

4. Went back home, Lord, my home was lonesome, since my mother, she was gone.
   All my brothers, sisters cryin', what a home so sad and 'lone.

Strumming (thumb lead):

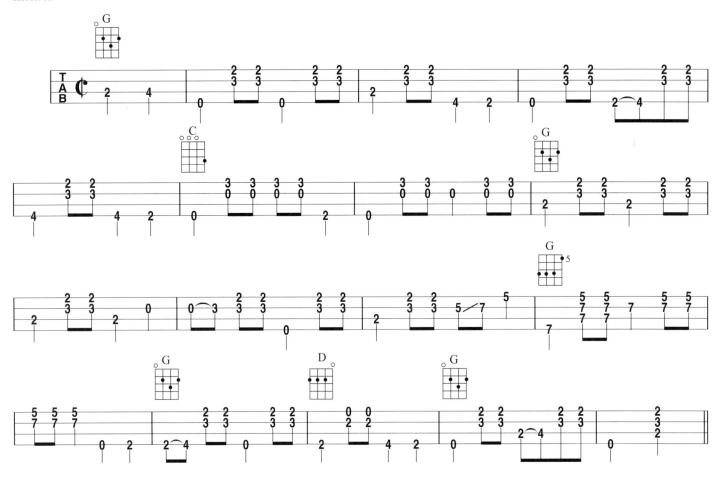

Rolling:

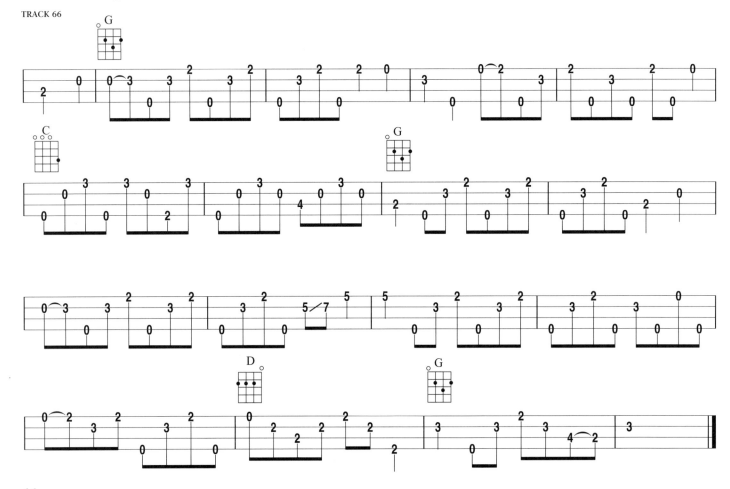

All The Good Times Are Past And Gone

TRACK 67

This old folk tune has long been a standard in bluegrass circles. Since it's the only waltz (3/4 time) song in this collection, it illustrates how to adapt strumming and roll-based picking to three beats per measure instead of four. Bars 7 and 8 of the strumming arrangement are typical examples of the 3/4 time strum (index finger lead).

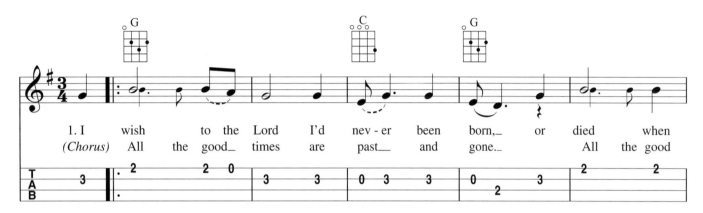

1. I wish to the Lord I'd nev-er been born,_ or died when
(Chorus) All the good_ times are past_ and gone._ All the good

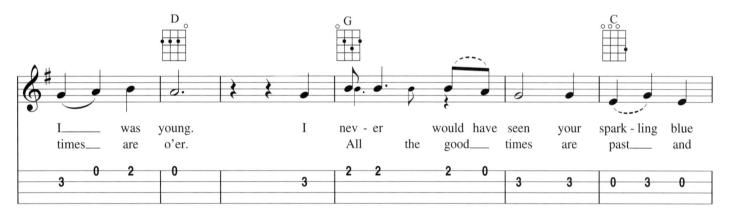

I_____ was young.   I nev-er would have seen your spark-ling blue
times_ are o'er.   All the good_ times are past_ and

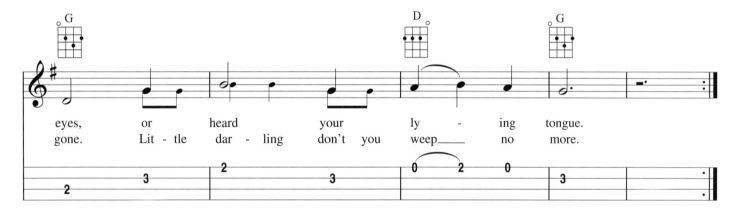

eyes,   or heard your ly - ing tongue.
gone.   Lit - tle dar - ling don't you weep_____ no more.

Additional Lyrics

2. Don't you see that passenger train coming around the bend?
   It's taking me away from this lonesome old town, never to return again.

3. Don't you see that lonesome dove flying from pine to pine?
   He's mourning for his own true love, just like I mourn for mine.

4. Come back, come back, my own true love and stay awhile with me.
   If ever I've had a friend in this world, you've been a friend to me.

Strumming (index lead):

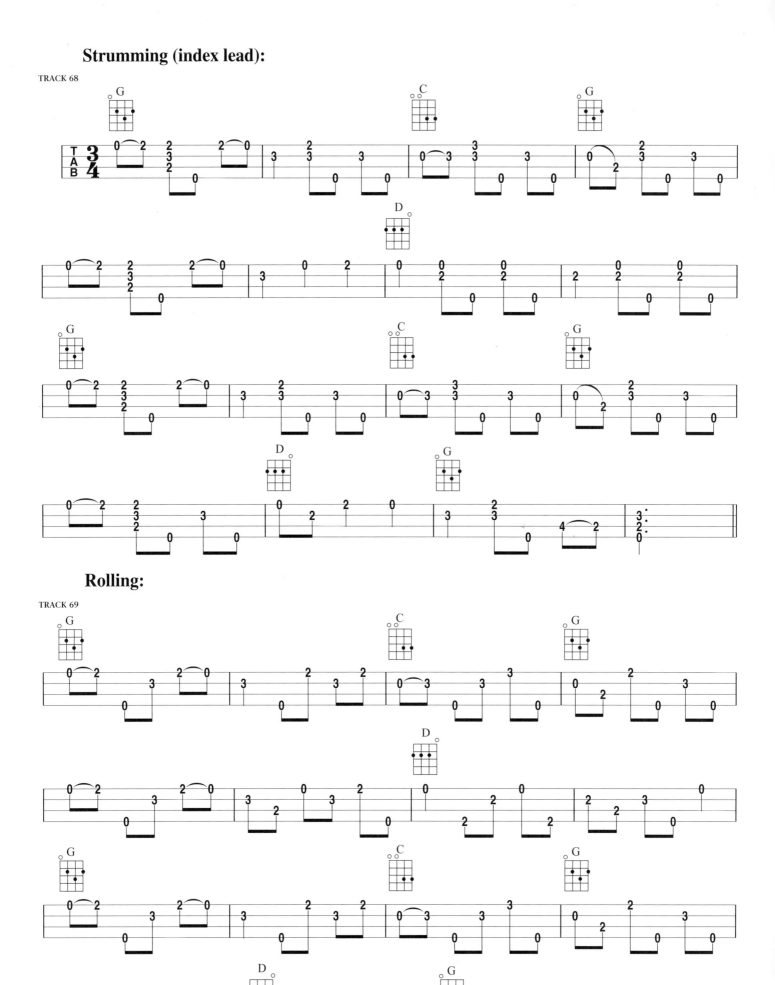

Rolling: